MUSIC & WORDS BY ELTON ROTH; CHANGES BY DAD

THIS GOSPEL SONG IS ABOUT 100 YEARS OLD &
   GETTING YOUNGER. HERE GOES;
I HAVE A DAUGHTER JESUS GAVE ME; SHE
 WAS SENT FROM HEAVEN ABOVE.
THERE NEVER WAS A SWEETER MELODIE; SHE'S
  A MELODIE OF LOVE.
                CHORUS

IN MY HEART THERE RINGS A MELODIE,
 THERE RINGS A MELODIE, WITH HEAVEN'S
HARMONY.
 IN MY HEART THERE RINGS A MELODIE;
THERE RINGS A MELODIE OF LOVE.

         Keep on ringing,

                Dad

❧

Presented to:

Melodie

By: Dad *

Date:

March 24, 2004

Occasion:

BIRTHDAY!

Watch this space!
* Poem will follow!

Warner Books, Inc., 1271 Avenue of the Americas, New York, NY 10020

Visit our website at www.twbookmark.com

ⓦ WARNER/*Faith* A Division of AOL Time Warner Book Group
The Warner Faith name and logo are registered trademarks of Warner Books, Inc.

Printed in the United States of America

First Printing: May 2003
10 9 8 7 6 5 4 3 2 1

ISBN: 0-446-53251-7
LCCN: 2003101825

THE SECRETS OF
SPIRITUAL POWER

Strength for Life's Battles

JOYCE MEYER

WARNER
Faith

Contents

BEHOLD YOUR GOD

God is always working in secret, behind the scenes, even when it feels as though nothing will ever change. For change to be lasting, it must come from the inside out. Only God can effect that type of heart change. Let God be God!

GOD'S WORD FOR YOU

What then shall we say to [all] this? If God is for us, who [can be] against us? [Who can be our foe, if God is on our side?]

ROMANS 8:31

Those who trust in, lean on, and confidently hope in the Lord are like Mount Zion, which cannot be moved but abides and stands fast forever.

As the mountains are round about Jerusalem, so the Lord is round about His people from this time forth and forever.

PSALM 125:1–2

one

BEHOLD YOUR GOD

od is a big God; nothing is impossible with Him. We have nothing to fear from our enemies because none of them are as great as our God.

God is for us; He is on our side. The devil has one position—he is against us. But God is over us, under us, through us, for us, and He surrounds us. Of whom, then, should we be afraid?

So like Mount Zion, we should never be moved because God is all around us. And if that wasn't enough, I saved the best until last: He is in us, and He said that He will never leave us or forsake us.

Salvation is our most awesome blessing from God, and we have been given the Helper, the Holy Spirit Himself, to empower us to be like Jesus. God has blessings and spiritual power in abundance for us. He is powerful and mighty and able to do what we can never do on our own.

God desires that we let the Holy Spirit flow through us in power to show people His love and to help people with His gifts. It all centers in Him.

God chooses the weak and foolish things of this world, on purpose, so that people may look at them and say, "It has to be God!"

GOD'S WORD FOR YOU

For we are not wrestling with flesh and blood [contending only with physical opponents], but against the despotisms, against the powers, against [the master spirits who are] the world rulers of this present darkness, against the spirit forces of wickedness in the heavenly (supernatural) sphere.

EPHESIANS 6:12

THE WARFARE WITHIN

In waging spiritual warfare with God's power, we must remember that we war against Satan and his demons, not against other people . . . and not with our own selves.

Probably the greatest war we wage is one we wage with ourselves about ourselves, struggling with where we are spiritually compared to where we see we need to be. We may struggle with feeling that we should have accomplished more in life than we have; we may feel we are a financial failure or many other things. But one thing is a fact: We can't change anything by being frustrated and struggling within. Only God can fight our battles and win. These internal battles are truly battles and must be handled the same way the rest of our battles are.

It is difficult to get to the place where we can be honest with ourselves about our sin and failures, our inabilities and fallibilities, and yet still know that we are right with God because Jesus made us right when He died for us and rose from the dead. If you are at war within yourself, knowing you are right with God is a tremendous key to tapping into spiritual power.

*We can be changed as we worship and behold God —
not as we look at ourselves, adding up our many flaws —
but as we look to Him.*

GOD'S WORD FOR YOU

But we all, with open face beholding as in a glass the glory of the Lord, are changed into the same image from glory to glory, even as by the Spirit of the Lord.

2 CORINTHIANS 3:18 KJV

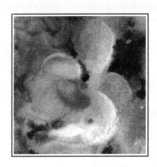

WE ARE CHANGING

I want to change, and I am sure you do also. I want to see changes in my behavior. I want to see regular progress. For example, I want more stability; I want to walk in a great measure of love and all the other fruit of the Spirit. I want to be kind and good to others, even if I don't feel good or am not having a particularly good day. Even when things are coming against me and things aren't working out the way I'd like, I still want to display the character of Jesus Christ.

Through the power of the Holy Spirit within us, we are able to be sweet, nice, and kind, even when things are not going our way. We are able to stay calm when everything around us seems topsy-turvy, when everything seems to be conspiring against us to cause us to lose our patience and get angry and upset.

The key for me has been to finally learn that God changes me through His grace, not through my struggles to change myself. I suffered many years of wrestling with myself before I discovered God's power to change me within—little by little.

This is how God changes us. He reveals something to us and then waits until we decide to trust Him with it before He works in us His character in that area.

GOD'S WORD FOR YOU

I am the Vine; you are the branches. Whoever lives in Me and I in him bears much (abundant) fruit. However, apart from Me [cut off from vital union with Me] you can do nothing.

JOHN 15:5

ONLY IN JESUS

I was a very independent person, and God began speaking John 15:5 to me early in my walk with Him. One of the spiritual laws of receiving spiritual power from God is entire dependence upon Him. Without faith we cannot please God. Faith involves the leaning of the entire human personality in absolute trust in God's power, wisdom, and goodness.

We are to lean on, rely only, and entirely depend on Him, taking all the weight off of ourselves and putting it all on Him. Without God's help, we can't change anything in our lives. We can't change ourselves, our spouse, our family, our friends, or our circumstances. Truly, apart from Him we cannot do anything!

We forfeit peace and joy when we fail to let God be God. We try to figure out things we have no business even touching with our minds. Nothing is too hard or too wonderful for God, but many things are too hard or too wonderful for us. We need to grow to the place where we rest in the fact that we know the One Who knows . . . and we're free to trust Him.

It is so liberating to say, "Lord, I don't know what to do, and even if I did, I couldn't do it. But my eyes are on You. I am going to wait and watch You work it all out."

GOD'S WORD FOR YOU

And all Judah stood before the Lord, with their children and their wives.

Then the Spirit of the Lord came upon Jahaziel son of Zechariah, the son of Benaiah, the son of Jeiel, the son of Mattaniah, a Levite of the sons of Asaph, in the midst of the assembly.

He said, Hearken, all Judah, you inhabitants of Jerusalem, and you King Jehoshaphat. The Lord says this to you: Be not afraid or dismayed at this great multitude; for the battle is not yours, but God's.

2 CHRONICLES 20:13–15

Wait on God

I love 2 Chronicles 20:13–15 because it is a power verse! King Jehoshaphat and the people were facing a vast army and impossible odds. But rather than take a natural action, Jehoshaphat took a spiritual action. In God's economy of spiritual power, waiting upon God and standing still is a spiritual action. In effect, he was saying, "Lord, I will wait upon You to deliver us. And I'm going to enjoy my life while I wait for You."

Satan hates our joy. He wants to see anger, unbridled emotions, tears, self-pity, grumbling, complaining, blaming God and others for our life situations. He wants to see anything but joy, because the joy of the Lord is our strength (Nehemiah 8:10). We need the strength we gain while waiting in order to do whatever it is God will instruct us to do when He gives us direction.

We are tempted to think we are not doing our part if we don't worry or try to figure out some answer, but this will prevent our deliverance rather than aid it. It is not irresponsible to enjoy life when we wait on the Lord to solve our problems (John 10:10).

God's answer was very plain and simple: Do not fear because the battle is not yours, but the Lord's.

GOD'S WORD FOR YOU

Tomorrow go down to them. Behold, they will come up by the Ascent of Ziz, and you will find them at the end of the ravine before the Wilderness of Jeruel.

You shall not need to fight in this battle; take your positions, stand still, and see the deliverance of the Lord [Who is] with you, O Judah and Jerusalem. Fear not nor be dismayed. Tomorrow go out against them, for the Lord is with you.

And Jehoshaphat bowed his head with his face to the ground, and all Judah and the inhabitants of Jerusalem fell down before the Lord, worshiping Him.

And some Levites of the Kohathites and Korahites stood up to praise the Lord, the God of Israel, with a very loud voice.

2 CHRONICLES 20:16–19

TAKE YOUR POSITION

The people of Judah did not only stand still before the Lord. When they heard the Lord's instruction, the king and the people bowed on their knees with their faces to the ground and worshiped. Wow! Worship was their actual position, and in worshiping they were also standing still. Kneeling in reverence before God is a battle position and a key to spiritual power.

To "praise" God means to ascribe to Him the glory due to His name. It means to talk about and sing out about the goodness, grace, and greatness of God. "To worship" is "to make obeisance, do reverence to, to serve." Broadly, it may be regarded as the direct acknowledgment to God, of His nature, attributes, ways, and claims, whether by the outgoing of the heart in praise and thanksgiving or by deed done in such an acknowledgment.

We must learn to fight God's way, not the world's way. Our battle position is one of worship. To stand means to abide or to enter God's rest. Our position in Christ is to worship and praise Him. We stand our ground and persist in believing that God will work in our life and circumstances. We refuse to give up.

As we worship the Lord, we release the emotional or mental burden that is weighing us down. It is swallowed up in the awesomeness of God.

GOD'S WORD FOR YOU

But those who wait for the Lord [who expect, look for, and hope in Him] shall change and renew their strength and power; they shall lift their wings and mount up [close to God] as eagles [mount up to the sun]; they shall run and not be weary, they shall walk and not faint or become tired.

ISAIAH 40:31

How Long, Lord?

By starting to worship God for the changes He is already working in us, we find that those changes start manifesting more and more. And we experience new levels of God's glory, which is the manifestation of all His excellencies. In other words, God will pour His goodness out upon the worshiper.

The amount of time the changes require in our lives is dependent upon (1) how long it takes us to get into agreement with God that we have the problem He says we have; (2) how long it takes us to stop making excuses and blaming it on someone else; (3) how long we spin our wheels, trying to change ourselves; (4) how much time we spend studying His Word, waiting on and worshiping Him, truly believing that He is working in us.

God is always trying to work in us. He calls Himself "I AM" and is ever present to change us. He is a gentleman and will not force His way into our lives; He must be invited. As we relax under His mighty hand, He begins to remold us into what His original intention was before the world messed us up. He will definitely do a good job, if we release ourselves into His mighty hand.

God can change you while you read this book,
if you will trust Him.

GOD'S WORD FOR YOU

So Ahab went up to eat and to drink. And Elijah went up to the top of Carmel; and he bowed himself down upon the earth and put his face between his knees

And said to his servant, Go up now, look toward the sea. And he went up and looked and said, There is nothing. Elijah said, Go again seven times.

And at the seventh time the servant said, A cloud as small as a man's hand is arising out of the sea. And Elijah said, Go up, say to Ahab, Hitch your chariot and go down, lest the rain stop you.

In a little while, the heavens were black with wind-swept clouds, and there was a great rain. And Ahab went to Jezreel.

1 KINGS 18:42–45

RELEASING GOD

God changes us from one degree of glory to another, but don't forget to enjoy the glory you are in right now while you are headed for the next one. Don't compare the glory you are in with the glory of someone else who appears to be in a greater degree of glory. Each of us is an individual, and God deals with us differently, according to what He knows we need.

You may not notice changes on a daily basis, but I want to stir your faith up so you will believe that God is at work, just as He said He would be. Remember, we see *after* we believe, not *before*. We struggle with ourselves because of all that we are not, when we should be praising and worshiping God for all that we are. As we worship Him for Who He is, we see things released into our lives that we could have never made happen ourselves.

As we worship God, we are released from frustration. All those pent-up, weird, emotional things that need to go begin to vanish. As we worship, God's character is released in our lives and begins to manifest.

We release God to work in our lives as we release our faith in Him. God's truth will set you free if you stick with God's battle plan, and you will like the results!

GOD'S WORD FOR YOU

For those whom He foreknew [of whom He was aware and loved beforehand], He also destined from the beginning [foreordaining them] to be molded into the image of His Son [and share inwardly His likeness], that He might become the firstborn among many brethren.

ROMANS 8:29

And Jesus called [to Him] the throng with His disciples and said to them, If anyone intends to come after Me, let him deny himself [forget, ignore, disown, and lose sight of himself and his own interests] and take up his cross, and [joining Me as a disciple and siding with My party] follow with Me [continually, cleaving steadfastly to Me].

MARK 8:34

CHRISTLIKENESS

Our number one goal in life as Christians should be Christlikeness. Jesus is the express image of the Father, and we are to follow in His footsteps. He came as the Pioneer of our faith to show us by example how we should live. We should seek to behave with people the way Jesus did. Our goal is not to see how successful we can be in business or how famous we can be. It is not prosperity, popularity, or even building a big ministry, but to be Christlike.

Spiritual maturity or Christlikeness cannot be obtained without "dying to self." That simply means saying yes to God and no to ourselves when our will and God's are in opposition. Jesus told His disciples that if they wanted to follow Him, they would need to take up their cross daily.

To follow Christ and become like Him, we must be willing to forget about what we want—our plans, having our own way—and instead trust Him to show us what His will is for us. His will always leads to deep joy and satisfaction, and the prize is well worth it!

The world is not impressed by our bumper stickers and Christian jewelry. They want to see fruit of godly behavior. They want to see lives energized by the Spirit of God that reflect the image of Jesus.

SUPERNATURAL
FAVOR

❧

The grace of God is the favor of God.
It is the supernatural power of God
coming through our faith to do what
we cannot do on our own.

GOD'S WORD FOR YOU

*Let us then fearlessly and confidently and boldly draw
near to the throne of grace (the throne of God's unmerited
favor to us sinners), that we may receive mercy [for our
failures] and find grace to help in good time for every need
[appropriate help and well-timed help, coming just when
we need it].*

HEBREWS 4:16

*Now to Him Who, by (in consequence of) the [action
of His] power that is at work within us, is able to [carry
out His purpose and] do superabundantly, far over and
above all that we [dare] ask or think [infinitely beyond our
highest prayers, desires, thoughts, hopes, or dreams] . . .*

EPHESIANS 3:20

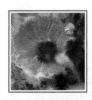

t w o

SUPERNATURAL FAVOR

hen I first started ministering, I was scared. I was afraid of being rejected. In those days, for a woman to do what I was doing was even less popular than it is today when women preachers are more widely accepted. So I bent over backward to speak and behave the way I thought was expected of me.

The problem was that I was trying to win natural favor, and it didn't and won't work. Trying to get favor on your own is not only hard work, it is often pointless. The harder you try, the less people are attracted to you.

At the time, I knew nothing about supernatural favor. I didn't know that favor is a part of grace. In fact, in the English New Testament the words *grace* and *favor* are both translated from the same Greek word *charis*. So the grace of God is the favor of God. And the grace of God causes things to happen in our life that need to happen, through the channel of our faith. It is the power of God coming through our faith to do what we cannot do on our own. It is not by human power, or by human might, but by the Holy Spirit that we receive favor. It is by God's Spirit of grace that we find favor with God and with man.

Once you believe God for supernatural favor,
it relieves the stress that builds up in you.
Rather than try to do everything for yourself,
you just do your best and leave the results to God.

29

GOD'S WORD FOR YOU

But He gives us more and more grace (power of the Holy Spirit, to meet this evil tendency and all others fully). That is why He says, God sets Himself against the proud and haughty, but gives grace [continually] to the lowly (those who are humble enough to receive it).

JAMES 4:6

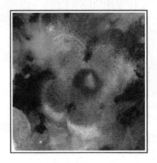

NATURAL FAVOR

I need to emphasize the distinction between natural favor and supernatural favor as it relates to spiritual power. Natural favor can be earned, whereas supernatural favor and power can't.

If you work hard enough and long enough, you can get people to like and accept you most of the time. But that acceptance must be maintained, and this is where so many people get into trouble. Saying and doing all the right things becomes a form of bondage.

God doesn't want us to spend our time and energy trying to earn favor with Him or with others. He wants us to devote our time and energy to walking in His supernatural favor through the Spirit and doing His will, whether it is popular or not. We cannot earn His favor; it is a pure gift from God. And the way we get it is simply by believing and receiving it from God.

This is why I pray daily for favor, supernatural favor. God gives grace to the humble, and it is my one desire that His spiritual power will freely flow through my life and words and actions.

When we know that everything we have and enjoy is a gift from God, a result of His supernatural favor upon us, then there is nothing left for us to do but say, "Thank You, Lord."

GOD'S WORD FOR YOU

And Joseph's master took him and put him in the prison, a place where the state prisoners were confined; so he was there in the prison.

But the Lord was with Joseph, and showed him mercy and loving-kindness and gave him favor in the sight of the warden of the prison.

And the warden of the prison committed to Joseph's care all the prisoners who were in the prison; and whatsoever was done there, he was in charge of it.

The prison warden paid no attention to anything that was in [Joseph's] charge, for the Lord was with him and made whatever he did to prosper.

GENESIS 39:20–23

THE FAITH ATTITUDE

Although Joseph was being punished unfairly because he was jailed for something he didn't do, the Lord was still with him in supernatural favor and took care of him. He proved that a person is really not in too bad a shape, even if he ends up in prison, if God gives him favor.

No matter what happens to us in life, we can have favor with God and with other people (Luke 2:52). But like so many good things in life, just because something is available to us does not mean that we will partake of it. The Lord makes many things available to us that we never receive and enjoy because we never activate our faith in that area.

For example, if we go to a job interview confessing fear and failure, we will almost be assured not to get the job. On the other hand, even if we apply for a job that we know we aren't fully qualified for, we can still go in confidence, believing that God will give us favor in every situation that is His will.

God wants to give you favor, but you must do what Joseph did and believe for it. Joseph maintained a good attitude in a bad situation. He had a "faith attitude," and God gave him favor.

GOD'S WORD FOR YOU

Now when the turn for Esther the daughter of Abihail, the uncle of Mordecai who had taken her as his own daughter, had come to go in to the king, she required nothing but what Hegai the king's attendant, the keeper of the women, suggested. And Esther won favor in the sight of all who saw her.

So Esther was taken to King Ahasuerus into his royal palace in the tenth month, the month of Tebeth, in the seventh year of his reign.

And the king loved Esther more than all the women, and she obtained grace and favor in his sight more than all the maidens, so that he set the royal crown on her head and made her queen instead of Vashti.

ESTHER 2:15–17

UNDER GOD'S CONTROL

Did you know there is a Scripture that says God brings one person down and lifts up another? You need to read 1 Samuel 2:7. One instance is the life of Esther. God raised her up from obscurity to become the queen of the entire land. He gave her favor with everyone she met, including the king, because she had found favor with God.

Later in the story, Esther drew upon that favor to save herself and her people, the Jews, from being murdered by the evil Haman, who was out to destroy them. She may have been afraid to go to the king and ask him to intervene, because doing so could have cost her very life, but she did because she trusted her life to God.

Whatever situation comes into your life, even if you are being harassed, persecuted, or discriminated against, or someone is trying to take something from you that rightfully belongs to you—whether it is your job, your home, your reputation, or anything in life— believe God for supernatural favor. Despite how hopeless things may look, God can lift up and He can bring down. If your life is in His hands, believe that the light of the Lord shines upon you to give you favor.

Don't go through life being afraid or harboring a fear of rejection. God's power will always see you through.

GOD'S WORD FOR YOU

And the [Babylonian] king told Ashpenaz, the master of his eunuchs, to bring in some of the children of Israel, both of the royal family and of the nobility. . . .

Among these were of the children of Judah: Daniel, Hananiah, Mishael, and Azariah.

The chief of the eunuchs gave them names: Daniel he called Belteshazzar [the king's attendant], Hananiah he called Shadrach, Mishael he called Meshach, and Azariah he called Abednego.

But Daniel determined in his heart that he would not defile himself by [eating his portion of] the king's rich and dainty food or by [drinking] the wine which he drank; therefore he requested of the chief of the eunuchs that he might [be allowed] not to defile himself.

Now God made Daniel to find favor, compassion, and loving-kindness with the chief of the eunuchs.

DANIEL 1:3, 6–9

OVER AND ABOVE

The story of Daniel and the Hebrew children may be a familiar story, but we must not miss the lesson of how God's supernatural favor was with them after being taken far from their homes and families.

Because of their sins against the Lord, the nation of Judah was carried away into captivity in Babylon. There, some of the most promising of them, including Daniel and three of his friends, were chosen to become attendants to the Babylonian king. As part of their three-year period of training, these young men were to follow a diet of rich meat and wine provided from the king's table. However, Daniel and his friends determined not to defile themselves with this diet and asked to be allowed to follow their own Hebrew diet.

They refused to compromise their convictions, and we are told that the Lord gave Daniel "favor, compassion, and loving-kindness" with the chief of eunuchs. They had permission to follow their own diet as long as it didn't harm them. Of course, not only did it not harm them, it made them stronger and healthier and led them to be chosen as trusted counselors.

Under God's favor and power, Daniel rose to become prime minister of the world's greatest power. What would have happened if he had not trusted God over and above all he asked or imagined?

GOD'S WORD FOR YOU

And Jesus increased in wisdom (in broad and full understanding) and in stature and years, and in favor with God and man.

LUKE 2:52

Now the centurion, having seen what had taken place, recognized God and thanked and praised Him, and said, Indeed, without question, this Man was upright (just and innocent)!

LUKE 23:47

FAVORED OF THE LORD

From childhood, Jesus walked in the supernatural favor of God and men. In fact, once He began His public ministry, He was so popular that He could hardly find time to get alone to pray and fellowship with His heavenly Father. Even those who did not believe in Him recognized that He enjoyed the favor of God. When the Pharisees sent guards to arrest Jesus, they went back saying, "Never has a man talked as this Man talks!" (John 7:46). Right up until the very end of His life, even on the cross, that special favor and power were recognized (Luke 23:47–48).

That is the way I would like for you and me to come to see ourselves, as the favored of the Lord. He doesn't see us as weak, helpless, sinful creatures. He sees us robed in righteousness, shod with the shoes of peace, wearing the full armor of God, and wielding the sword of the Spirit, which is the Word of the Lord. That is how we ought to see ourselves.

No matter how we may appear to ourselves or to others, we must never forget that God can cause the light of His favor to shine upon us—just as He did for Jesus—so that we too increase in wisdom and stature.

Stop looking at your life in the natural. You are not giving the Lord any credit for what He can do.

GOD'S WORD FOR YOU

And I will pour out upon the house of David and upon the inhabitants of Jerusalem the Spirit of grace or unmerited favor and supplication.

ZECHARIAH 12:10

THE MISSING LINK

The message of God's grace has been the single most important message that the Holy Spirit has ministered to me. My entire Christian experience was a struggle before I learned about the spiritual power of grace. To teach people faith and not teach them grace is, in my opinion, "the missing link" in many people's faith walk.

Grace is the power of the Holy Spirit that is available to do whatever needs to be done in our lives, the power to bring and sustain change. It is the ability of God that comes to us free for the asking. Through faith the grace of God is received. Faith is not the price that buys the blessings of God, but it is the hand that receives them.

Just hearing the word *grace* is soothing to me. Always remember that when you feel frustrated it is because you have entered into your own effort and need to get back into God's power. Grace leaves you strong and calm; works render you weak and powerless, frustrated and frantic. Don't be discouraged if change doesn't come as quickly as you'd like. It will take time.

Receive not only the grace that saves, but receive grace, grace, and more grace so you may live victoriously and glorify Jesus in your daily life.

GOD'S WORD FOR YOU

Now the Lord is the Spirit, and where the Spirit of the Lord is, there is liberty (emancipation from bondage, freedom).

2 CORINTHIANS 3:17

In [this] freedom Christ has made us free [and completely liberated us]; stand fast then, and do not be hampered and held ensnared and submit again to a yoke of slavery [which you have once put off].

GALATIANS 5:1

42

FREEDOM AND LIBERTY

Each of us would like to be favored or featured. Is that pride? No, not if that position comes from God and not from our own personal ambitions or our own selfish efforts to call attention to ourselves.

To be totally honest, I find it delightful to watch God feature a person. It is fun to watch Him single out someone for special attention or preferential treatment. To see Him work powerfully in someone's life provokes genuine praise and thanksgiving.

It is always enjoyable to have favor with God. It just seems that it doesn't happen as often as we would like. Part of the problem is us. We don't have nearly as much fun with the Lord as we should. We should have more freedom and liberty, and less fear and legalism. There are so many things that God would love to do for us, but He cannot because we won't ask. One reason we won't ask is because we don't feel worthy. The only time we will go to God and ask for special favor is when we are absolutely desperate.

It is time we believe the words of our Father: "You are the apple of My eye. You are My favorite child."

Our heavenly Father wants His children to stand up and be everything for which His Son, Jesus, gave His life that they might become.

GOD'S WORD FOR YOU

O Lord, our Lord, how excellent (majestic and glorious) is Your name in all the earth! You have set Your glory on [or above] the heavens.

Out of the mouths of babes and unweaned infants You have established strength because of Your foes, that You might silence the enemy and the avenger.

When I view and consider Your heavens, the work of Your fingers, the moon and the stars, which You have ordained and established,

What is man that You are mindful of him, and the son of [earthborn] man that You care for him?

Yet You have made him but a little lower than God [or heavenly beings], and You have crowned him with glory and honor.

You made him to have dominion over the works of Your hands; You have put all things under his feet . . .

PSALM 8:1–6

CROWNED WITH GLORY

If you notice in verse 5 of Psalm 8, God has chosen man and crowned him with glory and honor. Here, in my opinion, *honor* and *favor* have the same meaning. We might say that God has crowned man with glory and favor, giving him dominion over the works of His hand, and placing all things under his feet. I describe the word *glory* in this instance as the excellencies of God. And to be *crowned* symbolizes triumph and reward.

Just because we don't see a crown on our head doesn't mean there is none there. No matter what we feel, we have been crowned with God's favor and excellence. We were never meant to muddle our way through life, taking whatever the devil throws at us without claiming what is rightfully ours.

If you read verse 6, you will see that all things have been placed under our feet by God, Who has given us dominion over all His creation. By faith in the finished work of Jesus on the cross, we have all the spiritual power we need to prevent the devil and his demons from intimidating, dominating, and oppressing us. This is our right under God's favor.

We walk in our God-given glory and honor
only to the extent we determine to do so.
Learn to avail yourself of it and walk in it.

Be Transformed

*It is obvious that some people are closer
to God than others. Some people have a "close
friends" familiarity with God that seems
foreign to others. The truth is that each of us
is as close to God as we want to be.*

GOD'S WORD FOR YOU

One thing have I asked of the Lord, that will I seek, inquire for, and [insistently] require: that I may dwell in the house of the Lord [in His presence] all the days of my life, to behold and gaze upon the beauty [the sweet attractiveness and the delightful loveliness] of the Lord and to meditate, consider, and inquire in His temple.

PSALM 27:4

three

BE TRANSFORMED

I remember the emptiness I felt in 1976 when as a young Christian I realized that doing the right things brought temporary happiness but not deep, satisfying joy. My relationship with God was much like the Israelites', who could only see God from a distance while Moses talked with God face-to-face. God was very real to them, and they could hear His voice, but to them He looked like a consuming fire.

Perhaps you are experiencing what I went through. I lived by the law of the church, doing everything I was told to do, and expecting my routine of good works to bring the peace and joy and spiritual power the Scriptures promise. Instead, I found myself deeply disheartened that nothing seemed to be working. My life was full of irritations and aggravations that robbed me of true contentment. I knew I needed real change in my life, but I didn't know what I needed. I was searching, but I didn't know what I was searching for.

Many of us want the blessings and power of God, but we don't crave and pursue Him, or lay aside other things to go after a word from the Lord. We want to be transformed, but unlike David, we fail to commit ourselves to one thing—the manifest presence of God.

The only thing that truly satisfies the longing within is to know God more intimately today than we did yesterday.

GOD'S WORD FOR YOU

But He replied, It has been written, Man shall not live and be upheld and sustained by bread alone, but by every word that comes forth from the mouth of God.

MATTHEW 4:4

And do not get drunk with wine, for that is debauchery; but ever be filled and stimulated with the [Holy] Spirit.

EPHESIANS 5:18

A REALITY CHECK

I don't think there's anything better than just to be satisfied. To wake up in the morning and think, *Life is good, praise God, I'm satisfied,* and to go to bed at night still satisfied is truly living abundantly. On the other hand, I don't think there is anything much worse than living in a low-level state of dissatisfaction all the time.

Here is a spiritual reality check. No matter what you own, where you go, or what you do, nothing can give you true gratification besides the presence of God. Money, trips, vacations, clothes, new opportunities, new furniture and new houses, getting married and having children are all things that can give us a degree of happiness. But we will never be permanently, consistently satisfied if we seek things to own or do in order to quench the empty void inside us.

I am pressing this point because I know there are many unhappy believers who are without the knowledge of what to do about their dry, unfulfilled lives. Too many are missing out on the rich pleasure that comes from fellowshipping daily with the heavenly Father through the Holy Spirit. If that's true in your life, be honest with God and open your heart to Him.

If we are ever to have real victory,
you and I have to learn the simple scriptural truth:
We have not because we ask not.

GOD'S WORD FOR YOU

So I say to you, Ask and keep on asking and it shall be given you; seek and keep on seeking and you shall find; knock and keep on knocking and the door shall be opened to you.

For everyone who asks and keeps on asking receives; and he who seeks and keeps on seeking finds; and to him who knocks and keeps on knocking, the door shall be opened.

What father among you, if his son asks for a loaf of bread, will give him a stone; or if he asks for a fish, will instead of a fish give him a serpent?

Or if he asks for an egg, will give him a scorpion?

If you then, evil as you are, know how to give good gifts [gifts that are to their advantage] to your children, how much more will your heavenly Father give the Holy Spirit to those who ask and continue to ask Him!

LUKE 11:9–13

FILLED WITH THE SPIRIT

On a Friday morning in February 1976, I was driving to work and feeling discouraged. Nothing in my life seemed to be working right, despite my best attempts. Out of sheer frustration and desperation I cried out to God that I couldn't go on any longer with the way things were. I was like a starving person, so spiritually hungry I was ready to receive anything as long as I knew it was from God. I was totally open to God.

To my surprise God spoke to me in the car that morning. He called my name and spoke to me about patience. I knew with certainty that God was going to do something in my life, although I didn't know what He would do or when.

After work, I was sitting at a red light, and I felt my heart fill with faith about what God was going to do. I began to thank Him for it, and at that very moment, Jesus filled me with the presence of the Holy Spirit in a way I had never experienced. It felt as if someone had poured me full of liquid love, and it had such a profound effect upon my behavior that people began asking me what had happened. I was peaceful, happy, and easy to get along with—truly changed!

We are to seek the Lord, and not the experience of another person. He alone decides how and exactly when to manifest His presence in our lives.

GOD'S WORD FOR YOU

And having said this, He breathed on them and said to them, Receive the Holy Spirit!

JOHN 20:22

And while being in their company and eating at the table with them, He commanded them not to leave Jerusalem but to wait for what the Father had promised, Of which [He said] you have heard Me speak.

For John baptized with water, but not many days from now you shall be baptized with (placed in, introduced into) the Holy Spirit. . . .

But you shall receive power (ability, efficiency, and might) when the Holy Spirit has come upon you, and you shall be My witnesses in Jerusalem and all Judea and Samaria and to the ends (the very bounds) of the earth.

ACTS 1:4–5, 8

*I*MMERSED IN THE SPIRIT

Before Jesus was taken up into heaven after He was resurrected from the dead (Acts 1:3), He gathered the disciples and told them not to leave Jerusalem but to wait for the coming outpouring of the Holy Spirit. These were the same disciples whom Jesus had previously breathed upon and told to receive the Holy Spirit. I believe this was when they were born again. So if the disciples had already received the Holy Spirit, which they had, why were they told to await the baptism of the Holy Spirit?

When we are born again, we have the Holy Spirit *in* us. Acts 1:8 promises that He will also come *upon* us with power to be Christ's witnesses to the ends of the earth. Not only do we enjoy the indwelling presence of God's Spirit through salvation, but we can receive His power to fill us in order to demonstrate His glory to the lost people around us.

A person may have a desire to do something and yet not have the power to perform it. In my life, it was only after I had been immersed in the Holy Spirit that I found the true desire to do God's will and the power to do it. It's the difference between doing and being.

There are countless things we struggle with when we could be receiving help from the divine Helper.

GOD'S WORD FOR YOU

Then Jesus came from Galilee to the Jordan to John to be baptized by him. . . .

And when Jesus was baptized, He went up at once out of the water; and behold, the heavens were opened, and he [John] saw the Spirit of God descending like a dove and alighting on Him.

MATTHEW 3:13, 16

How God anointed and consecrated Jesus of Nazareth with the [Holy] Spirit and with strength and ability and power; how He went about doing good and, in particular, curing all who were harassed and oppressed by [the power of] the devil, for God was with Him.

ACTS 10:38

ANOINTED WITH THE SPIRIT

Although Jesus was Himself God Who became flesh (John 1:1–14), we know that He laid aside His divine privileges to assume the guise of a servant in that He became like men and was born a human being (Philippians 2:6–7). Then He demonstrated the steps He wanted us to follow.

Before Jesus' public ministry began, He was anointed with the Holy Spirit and power. The description of the Holy Spirit's descent upon Jesus indicates that the Spirit permanently remained with Him (John 1:32).

For the Holy Spirit to reside with Jesus is significant because under the Old Covenant the Spirit came upon people for specific tasks but did not permanently remain on them. After the Spirit's descent, Jesus was led by the Spirit to be tempted by the devil and passed every test. Then He began His preaching ministry, which included miracles and other mighty acts empowered by the Holy Spirit.

When you are filled with the Holy Spirit, you are equipped for service in the kingdom of God. You receive the power that enables you to do what God wants you to do.

*If Jesus needed to be baptized by the Holy Spirit,
don't we need the same?*

GOD'S WORD FOR YOU

Then he fell to the ground, and heard a voice saying to him, "Saul, Saul, why are you persecuting Me?"

And he said, "Who are You, Lord?" Then the Lord said, "I am Jesus, whom you are persecuting. It is hard for you to kick against the goads."

So he, trembling and astonished, said, "Lord, what do You want me to do?" Then the Lord said to him, "Arise and go into the city, and you will be told what you must do."

ACTS 9:4–6 NKJV

So Ananias left and went into the house. And he laid his hands on Saul and said, Brother Saul, the Lord Jesus, Who appeared to you along the way by which you came here, has sent me that you may recover your sight and be filled with the Holy Spirit.

ACTS 9:17

58

THE TRANSFORMATION OF PAUL

Many say that believers receive everything they will ever get or need when they accept Jesus as Savior. That may be the case with some believers, but certainly not all. Different people have different experiences. I am not denying that some may be born again and baptized with the Holy Spirit at the same time; but others are not, and Paul was one of them.

When Paul (formerly called Saul) encountered the glorified Christ on the road to Damascus (Acts 9), he was persecuting Christians at the time, believing he was doing God a service. This was the moment of Paul's conversion, the time of his surrender as he called Jesus "Lord" and obeyed His instructions.

Three days later, the Lord spoke to a disciple named Ananias in a vision to go and pray for Paul. Despite the evil Paul had done, Ananias is told that Paul is a chosen instrument to bring the Gospel to the Gentiles and descendants of Israel. When Ananias laid his hands on Paul, Paul's eyes were opened, he was filled with the Holy Spirit, and then he went to be baptized in water. To say that his life changed forever at that moment is an understatement.

If the apostle Paul needed to be filled with the Holy Spirit, don't we need the same?

GOD'S WORD FOR YOU

[That you may really come] to know [practically, through experience for yourselves] the love of Christ, which far surpasses mere knowledge [without experience]; that you may be filled [through all your being] unto all the fullness of God [may have the richest measure of the divine Presence, and become a body wholly filled and flooded with God Himself]!

EPHESIANS 3:19

RECEIVING THE HOLY SPIRIT

I've focused on the baptism of the Holy Spirit because it is your personal key to spiritual power. Reading all this information will be of very little value to you unless you receive the Holy Spirit into your life. Spiritual power is an empty concept apart from Him.

To be filled with the Spirit, we must first have a desire. I believe that God often does not answer our first cries because He wants us to get desperate enough to be totally open to whatever He wants to do in our life. If you are truly hungry for more of God in your life, you are a candidate for the Spirit's baptism.

Receiving the Holy Spirit in our life is a holy thing, to be reverenced and even feared in a respectful way. God does not endue us with His power just for fun and games. He is a God of purpose, and all that He does in our life is for a purpose. Finding God's purpose and allowing Him to equip us for it should be the primary quest in our lives.

If you have this holy desire, God will meet you where you are. Open the door of your heart by stretching your faith out to God. Humble yourself and be prepared to obey whatever God asks of you.

Answer that knock at your heart's door and allow the Holy Spirit to come into your life in all His fullness.

GOD'S WORD FOR YOU

You do not have, because you do not ask.

JAMES 4:2

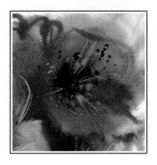

Ask and Receive

If you have read this far, it is now time to ask. Remember, the Holy Spirit will fill you, but only if invited to do so (Luke 11:13). Come boldly and ask. Ask fully expecting to receive. Don't be double-minded. Don't listen to doubt. Ask in faith. Believe you will receive, and you will receive. God is not a man that He should lie. He is faithful to fulfill His Word.

I had a definite experience of feeling the Spirit being poured into me. Since then, I have ministered the baptism of the Holy Spirit to literally thousands of people, and I have seen people react in every way. Many people do not feel a thing. Our experience cannot be based on feelings, but rather on faith.

Here is a prayer you might want to use: "Father, in Jesus' name, I ask You to baptize me in the power of the Holy Spirit with the evidence of speaking in tongues. Grant me boldness as You did those who were filled on the Day of Pentecost and give me other gifts that You desire me to have. Amen."

Wait on God quietly and believe that you are receiving. Don't try to make something happen. Let God minister to your spirit. To speak in tongues, open your mouth, and as the Spirit gives you utterance, speak forth what you hear coming up from your spirit. Give yourself totally to the Lord and trust Him as never before.

GOD'S WORD FOR YOU

*And when the day of Pentecost had fully come, they
were all assembled together in one place,*

*When suddenly there came a sound from heaven like
the rushing of a violent tempest blast, and it filled the whole
house in which they were sitting.*

*And there appeared to them tongues resembling fire,
which were separated and distributed and which settled on
each one of them.*

*And they were all filled (diffused throughout their souls)
with the Holy Spirit and began to speak in other (different,
foreign) languages (tongues), as the Spirit kept giving them
clear and loud expression [in each tongue in appropriate words].*

ACTS 2:1–4

EVIDENCE OF THE BAPTISM

The most important evidences of the Spirit-filled life are a character change and the development of the fruit of the Holy Spirit. Man is baptized by the Holy Spirit to enable him to live fully for God. Speaking in tongues was one of the evidences at Pentecost, but the most important evidence then was, and always will be, changed men and women.

The baptism of the Spirit changed Peter suddenly from a fearful man into an incredibly bold man. It transformed all the disciples of Jesus. We've already seen its effect in the life of Paul. It changed me, and it continues to change earnest seekers the world over.

Speaking in tongues is also an evidence, and it is a very valuable gift. I believe that the first outpouring on the Day of Pentecost is a pattern for the church to follow, and *all* of them spoke with other tongues.

I believe many people are baptized with the Holy Spirit and don't speak in tongues. I don't believe it is because they can't, but perhaps because they have been taught not to or perhaps they don't want the stigma that has unfortunately been attached to this gift. I beg you not to be afraid of God's good gift.

*Outer power only comes from inner purity
that transforms us into new men and women.*

LIFE IN
THE SPIRIT

*If you truly want to experience
the life of the Spirit as God intended,
then you must continually open every area
of your heart for Him to keep transforming
you by His power.*

GOD'S WORD FOR YOU

And we are setting these truths forth in words not taught by human wisdom but taught by the [Holy] Spirit, combining and interpreting spiritual truths with spiritual language [to those who possess the Holy Spirit].

1 CORINTHIANS 2:13

four

LIFE IN THE SPIRIT

was taught that the baptism in the Holy Spirit, speaking in tongues and the other gifts of the Spirit, and signs and wonders had passed away with the early church. Sadly, that is almost an accurate statement, but that was never God's will, nor His intention. He has always had a remnant of people somewhere in the earth who still believe in everything the Bible teaches, and it has been through that remnant that He has kept the truth alive.

If you have been one of the people who have not believed in these things, please read on and examine for yourself the Word of God. Most people are a little afraid of things they don't understand. We don't understand the supernatural realm, yet we are created by God in such a way that we hunger for it. We all have an interest in the supernatural, and if our need is not met by God, Satan will attempt to give us a counterfeit.

God gave me an awesome experience with the baptism in the Holy Spirit, and I was filled to overflowing. That was over twenty-five years ago, and I have never been the same since. God will do the same for you if you ask Him.

Life in the Spirit will bring you a closer fellowship and intimacy with God than you have ever known before.

GOD'S WORD FOR YOU

And afterward I will pour out My Spirit upon all flesh; and your sons and your daughters shall prophesy, your old men shall dream dreams, your young men shall see visions.

Even upon the menservants and upon the maidservants in those days will I pour out My Spirit.

JOEL 2:28–29

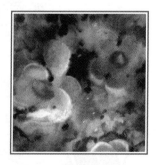

ℒife Under the New Covenant

The Old Covenant was a covenant of works, based on doing everything ourselves—struggling, striving, and laboring to be acceptable to God. It leaves us trapped in the works of the flesh. That kind of covenant steals our joy and peace.

But remember that the New Covenant is a covenant of grace, which is not based on what we can do, but what Christ has already done for us. Therefore, we are justified by our faith, not our works. That is so wonderful because it takes the pressure off us to perform. We can give up our outward efforts and allow God to work through us by the power of His Holy Spirit within us.

The bottom line is, the Old Covenant brings us bondage; the New Covenant brings us liberty. The infilling with the Holy Spirit is different from anything else we may experience. It enables us to *be* what we are supposed to be for God and then *do* what we are supposed to do.

Life in the Spirit is an awesome journey of living in the presence of God and being satisfied with God Himself.

God wants to bring a refreshing into your life,
like a mighty wind. Don't be poverty-stricken
in your soul when the answer is living inside you.

GOD'S WORD FOR YOU

For it is by free grace (God's unmerited favor) that you are saved (delivered from judgment and made partakers of Christ's salvation) through [your] faith. And this [salvation] is not of yourselves [of your own doing, it came not through your own striving], but it is the gift of God;

Not because of works [not the fulfillment of the Law's demands], lest any man should boast. [It is not the result of what anyone can possibly do, so no one can pride himself in it or take glory to himself.]

EPHESIANS 2:8–9

THE SPIRIT OF GRACE

Hebrews 10:29 tells us that it is "the [Holy] Spirit [Who imparts] grace (the unmerited favor and blessing of God)."

Grace is the power of the Holy Spirit available to you to do with ease what you cannot do by striving. But first, it is the power that enables you to be right with God so that you will become His home, the home of the Holy Spirit. With the Holy Spirit inside you, you can reach *in* to draw on the power of the Spirit of grace to do what you cannot do by striving in your own power.

The Holy Spirit ministers grace to us from God the Father. Grace is actually the Holy Spirit's power flowing out from the throne of God toward people to save them and enable them to live holy lives and accomplish the will of God.

There is no rejoicing in life without grace. With the grace of God, life can be lived with an effortless ease that produces an abundance of peace and joy.

When God makes the changes, God gets the glory. He won't let us change ourselves. We simply need to ask Him to change us and let His grace do its work in us.

GOD'S WORD FOR YOU

If you are censured and suffer abuse [because you bear] the name of Christ, blessed [are you—happy, fortunate, to be envied, with life-joy, and satisfaction in God's favor and salvation, regardless of your outward condition], because the Spirit of glory, the Spirit of God, is resting upon you. On their part He is blasphemed, but on your part He is glorified.

1 PETER 4:14

THE SPIRIT OF GLORY

Peter states that the Spirit of God, the Spirit of glory, rests upon us when we are reproached for the Name of Christ. We think it is awful when people mistreat us because we are Christians, but God sees it in an entirely different light. God never expects us to suffer for Him without His help. We can firmly believe that any time we are reproached or mistreated in any way because of our faith in Christ, God gives us an extra measure of His Spirit to counterbalance the attack. There is power to overcome.

When we have the Spirit of God in our lives, we can go through difficult circumstances and keep our peace and joy. Like Shadrach, Meshach, and Abednego in Daniel 3:21–27, we can go into the fiery furnace, or into problems and struggles, and come out without even the smell of smoke upon us.

When God's glory is manifested in your life, others will look at you and say, "Wow, what a great God you serve," because the power of His goodness toward you is visually evident to them. God wants to "Wow" you and them even more!

Welcome the Spirit of glory into your life and get excited about seeing the glory of God rise upon you in your difficult circumstances of life.

GOD'S WORD FOR YOU

Thus it is written, The first man Adam became a living being (an individual personality); the last Adam (Christ) became a life-giving Spirit [restoring the dead to life].

But it is not the spiritual life which came first, but the physical and then the spiritual.

The first man [was] from out of earth, made of dust (earthly-minded); the second Man [is] the Lord from out of heaven.

Now those who are made of the dust are like him who was first made of the dust (earthly-minded); and as is [the Man] from heaven, so also [are those] who are of heaven (heavenly-minded).

And just as we have borne the image [of the man] of dust, so shall we and so let us also bear the image [of the Man] of heaven.

1 CORINTHIANS 15:45–49

THE SPIRIT OF LIFE

When God created Adam, he lay on the ground a lifeless form until God breathed into him the breath of life, and he became a living soul. First Corinthians 15:45 says, "The first man Adam became a living being (an individual personality). . . ." Adam walked beside God, talked to Him, and believed in Him.

That verse goes on to say that Jesus, "the last Adam (Christ) became a life-giving Spirit [restoring the dead to life]." God gives us a physical life first, and then a spiritual. This spiritual rebirth is given to those who place their trust in God, believing that Jesus paid the price for sin and died for those who sincerely repent of their sins, change their minds for the better, and amend their ways.

When we accept Christ as our Savior, the Spirit of life comes to dwell within us, and we are quickened and made alive in our spirit. He has come that we may experience a life filled with the power of the Spirit of God, or a heavenly minded life as the life Jesus lived.

Jesus is the Light of the World, and His Spirit is the Spirit of life that swallows up death and all that tries to defeat us.

GOD'S WORD FOR YOU

But when He, the Spirit of Truth (the Truth-giving Spirit) comes, He will guide you into all the Truth (the whole, full Truth). For He will not speak His own message [on His own authority]; but He will tell whatever He hears [from the Father; He will give the message that has been given to Him], and He will announce and declare to you the things that are to come [that will happen in the future].

JOHN 16:13

THE SPIRIT OF TRUTH

In John 16:13, Jesus Himself refers to the Holy Spirit as the Spirit of Truth. The Holy Spirit was sent to guide us into all truth after Jesus' departure into heaven after His death, burial, and resurrection. In the previous verse, Jesus told His disciples, "I have still many things to say to you, but you are not able to bear them or to take them upon you or to grasp them now." He told them that the Holy Spirit would continue revealing things to them as they became ready to receive them.

We live in a world today that is filled with people who are living false lives, wearing masks of pretense and hiding things. That is wrong. But the reason it happens is that people have not been taught how to walk in the truth. You don't have to be afraid of truth. God won't bring revelation to you by His Spirit until He knows you are ready.

When the Spirit of Truth convicts us of sin, we need to turn that word back to Him and depend upon Him to give us the power to change it. The key to holiness is not pressure to perform but power to live.

If you are brave enough and wise enough to welcome the Spirit of Truth into every area of your life, you are in for a journey that you will never forget.

GOD'S WORD FOR YOU

So too the [Holy] Spirit comes to our aid and bears us up in our weakness; for we do not know what prayer to offer nor how to offer it worthily as we ought, but the Spirit Himself goes to meet our supplication and pleads in our behalf with unspeakable yearnings and groanings too deep for utterance.

And He Who searches the hearts of men knows what is in the mind of the [Holy] Spirit [what His intent is], because the Spirit intercedes and pleads [before God] in behalf of the saints according to and in harmony with God's will.

ROMANS 8:26–27

THE SPIRIT OF SUPPLICATION

According to Zechariah 12:10, the Holy Spirit is the Spirit of supplication. That means He is the Spirit of prayer. Each time we sense a desire to pray, it is the Holy Spirit giving us the desire. We may not realize how often the Holy Spirit is leading us to pray. We may just wonder why we have a certain person or situation on our mind so much. We frequently think of someone, and instead of praying, we keep thinking.

Recognizing when we are being led by the Holy Spirit to pray is often a lesson that takes a long time to learn. This is because we attribute far too many things to coincidence or chance rather than realizing that God is attempting to lead us by His Spirit.

When God gives us a burden to pray for someone, He wants to use us as His ministers and representatives, but we must learn to be more sensitive to the Spirit of supplication. The Holy Spirit not only leads us to pray, He helps us to pray. He shows us how to pray when we don't know what to pray for.

Welcome the Spirit of supplication into your life and allow the ministry of prayer to be fulfilled through you. It is quite wonderful to watch the miraculous things that take place in response to prayer.

GOD'S WORD FOR YOU

*For [the Spirit which] you have now received [is] not a
spirit of slavery to put you once more in bondage to fear,
but you have received the Spirit of adoption [the Spirit
producing sonship] in [the bliss of] which we cry, Abba
(Father)! Father!*

ROMANS 8:15

*But God—so rich is He in His mercy! Because of and
in order to satisfy the great and wonderful and intense love
with which He loved us,*

*Even when we were dead (slain) by [our own]
shortcomings and trespasses, He made us alive together in
fellowship and in union with Christ; [He gave us the very
life of Christ Himself, the same new life with which He
quickened Him, for] it is by grace (His favor and mercy
which you did not deserve) that you are saved (delivered
from judgment and made partakers of Christ's salvation).*

EPHESIANS 2:4–5

THE SPIRIT OF ADOPTION

The apostle Paul teaches us that the Holy Spirit is the Spirit of adoption. The word *adoption* means that we are brought into the family of God, even though we were previously outsiders, unrelated to God in any way. We were sinners serving Satan, but God in His great mercy redeemed us and purchased us with the blood of His own Son.

We understand adoption in the natural sense. We know that some children without parents are adopted by people who purposely choose them and take them as their own. What an honor to be chosen on purpose by those who want to pour out their love on them.

This is exactly what God did for us as believers in Christ. Because of what Jesus did for us on the cross, we are now eternally part of His family, and His Spirit dwells in our spirit and cries out to the Father. God the Father decided before the foundation of the world was laid that anyone who loved Christ would be loved and accepted by Him as His child. He decided He would adopt all those who accepted Jesus as their Savior. We become heirs of God and joint heirs with His Son, Jesus Christ.

It is the knowledge of our family relationship to God that gives us boldness to go before His throne and let our requests be made known.

GOD'S WORD FOR YOU

And [as to His divine nature] according to the Spirit
of holiness was openly designated the Son of God in power
[in a striking, triumphant and miraculous manner] by His
resurrection from the dead, even Jesus Christ our Lord
(the Messiah, the Anointed One).

ROMANS 1:4

THE SPIRIT OF HOLINESS

The Holy Spirit is called that because He is the holiness of God and because it is His job to work that holiness in all those who believe in Jesus Christ as Savior.

In 1 Peter 1:15–16, we are told: "But as the One Who called you is holy, you yourselves also be holy in all your conduct and manner of living. For it is written, You shall be holy, for I am holy." God would never tell us to be holy without giving us the help we need to make us that way. An unholy spirit could never make us holy, so God sends His Holy Spirit into our heart to do a complete and thorough work in us. The Holy Spirit will continue to work in us as long as we are on this earth. God hates sin, and anytime He finds it in us, He quickly works to cleanse us of it.

The Holy Spirit is also the Spirit of judgment and of burning, which relates to His being the Spirit of holiness. He judges sin in us and burns it out of us. It is not pleasant work as far as our feelings are concerned, but it eventually brings us into the state God desires us to be so that we may glorify Him.

Don't be a compromising Christian who has one foot in the world and one foot in the kingdom of God. Rather, be on fire for God, allowing His Spirit of holiness to refine you as pure gold.

CHANGED INTO HIS LIKENESS

We are to be living epistles read
of all men. We are to be lights shining
out brightly in a dark world. In order
to do that, we have to be people
of integrity, people of character,
people molded into the image of Jesus.

GOD'S WORD FOR YOU

*God said, Let Us [Father, Son, and Holy Spirit]
make mankind in Our image, after Our likeness, and
let them have complete authority over the fish of the sea,
the birds of the air, the [tame] beasts, and over all of the
earth, and over everything that creeps upon the earth.*

GENESIS 1:26

*My little children, for whom I am again suffering birth
pangs until Christ is completely and permanently formed
(molded) within you . . .*

GALATIANS 4:19

five

CHANGED INTO HIS LIKENESS

hen God said, "Let Us make man in Our image," this image does not refer to a physical likeness, but to character likeness. He meant that we were going to take on His nature, His character, as reflected in His Son, Jesus. It is to the degree that we are transformed into His image and likeness that spiritual power flows into and through our lives to the world around us.

The greatest goal of every believer should be Christlikeness. It is our highest calling in life. We should want the spiritual power within our lives to be able to handle situations the way Jesus would handle them and to treat people the way He would treat them. We should want to do things the way He would do them.

Jesus is our example. In John 13:15, He told His disciples, after washing their feet as a servant, "For I have given you this as an example, so that you should do [in your turn] what I have done to you." Peter tells us in 1 Peter 2:21: "For even to this were you called [it is inseparable from your vocation]. For Christ also suffered for you, leaving you [His personal] example, so that you should follow in His footsteps." May we humble ourselves as we seek to follow in those magnificent footsteps.

God is going to keep working with each of us until we get to the place where we act the way Jesus would act in every situation in life.

GOD'S WORD FOR YOU

And I am convinced and sure of this very thing, that He Who began a good work in you will continue until the day of Jesus Christ [right up to the time of His return], developing [that good work] and perfecting and bringing it to full completion in you.

PHILIPPIANS 1:6

MOLDED INTO HIS IMAGE

According to the Bible, God is the Potter, and we are the clay (Romans 9:20–21). We are like a hard, cold lump of clay that is not very pliable or easy to work with. But He puts us on His potter's wheel and begins to refashion and remake us because He doesn't like what we have become.

Sometimes that process of molding is very painful to us. The reason it hurts so much is that we do not fit the mold into which God is trying to fit us. So God keeps working and working on us, trimming away this bad attitude and that wrong mind-set, carefully remolding and reshaping us until gradually we are changed into the likeness of His Son.

Don't be discouraged with yourself because you have not yet arrived. You can walk in spiritual power as long as you maintain an attitude of pressing on. As long as you do your best to cooperate with God, He is pleased with you. Enjoy your life in the Spirit right now on the way to where God is shaping you. Let the Potter do His work of changing you from glory to glory.

God does not want us to be moldy; He wants us to be molded. Molded into the image of His Son. Remember, God will be shaping us right up until the time that Jesus returns to the earth!

GOD'S WORD FOR YOU

Moreover [let us also be full of joy now!] let us exult and triumph in our troubles and rejoice in our sufferings, knowing that pressure and affliction and hardship produce patient and unswerving endurance.

And endurance (fortitude) develops maturity of character (approved faith and tried integrity). And character [of this sort] produces [the habit of] joyful and confident hope of eternal salvation.

Such hope never disappoints or deludes or shames us, for God's love has been poured out in our hearts through the Holy Spirit Who has been given to us.

ROMANS 5:3–5

CHARACTER DEVELOPMENT

God wants to restore all of our character to godliness. Habit is actually character.

Habits are formed by discipline or the lack of discipline. Our character is basically what we do over and over. It is what other people have come to expect of us, such as being on time or how we respond in a certain circumstance. They know they can count or not count on us in this area. Over time, habits become part of our character.

We should not get legalistic about our character issues, but we do need to make an effort to develop character in those areas where we know we have problems. Changes in character come about by developing new habits. We need to commit ourselves to changing these faulty habits every time we confront them.

Godly character has much to do with discipline and the habits we form. Just as you can develop the habit of being on time, you can develop the habit of listening or giving to other people. You can choose to be kind and gentle, to curtail your spending, to watch your words, to pray, and to give thanks. It's about all of your life being shaped into the image of Christ.

God's power flows through faithful people, those who are faithful in the wilderness as well as the Promised Land.

GOD'S WORD FOR YOU

He was guilty of no sin, neither was deceit (guile)
ever found on His lips.
When He was reviled and insulted, He did not revile
or offer insult in return; [when] He was abused and suffered,
He made no threats [of vengeance]; but he trusted [Himself
and everything] to Him Who judges fairly.

1 PETER 2:22–23

94

CHARISMA IS NOT CHARACTER

According to Webster, one definition of *charisma* is "great personal magnetism: CHARM," but *character* is "moral or ethical strength: INTEGRITY." There are a lot of people who have charisma, but no character. Many people have a charming gift that can take them places where their character cannot keep them. We see this all the time in life and in the church.

Our character is revealed by what we do when nobody is watching. This was a key issue in my life and is a key to walking in spiritual power with God. Many people will do the right thing when somebody is watching them, but they won't do the right thing when nobody sees but God. As Christians, our commitment should be, "I am going to do the right thing simply because it is right."

Character is also seen when we do the right thing to others even though the right thing is not yet happening to us. As demonstrated by Jesus, one test of our character is, will we treat somebody right who is not treating us right? Will we bless someone who is not blessing us? It all comes down to what's in our heart, whether we trust Him Who judges fairly.

Our character is seen in how much strength we have to do the right thing even when we don't want to do it.

GOD'S WORD FOR YOU

The integrity of the upright shall guide them, but the willful contrariness and crookedness of the treacherous shall destroy them.

PROVERBS 11:3

Arise [from the depression and prostration in which circumstances have kept you—rise to a new life]! Shine (be radiant with the glory of the Lord), for your light has come, and the glory of the Lord has risen upon you!

For behold, darkness shall cover the earth, and dense darkness [all] peoples, but the Lord shall arise upon you [O Jerusalem], and His glory shall be seen on you.

ISAIAH 60:1–2

PERSONAL INTEGRITY

We live in a society that has so lost its sense of moral values that common decency is often not even practiced. Our world no longer honors God and is not concerned about integrity. Whether it involves cheating or committing fraud or speaking half-truths and exaggerations that lead others to believe something that is not true, our culture is saturated with the lies of the enemy.

As believers, we live in the world but are not to be of the world (John 17:11, 14). If we want to walk in spiritual power, we cannot compromise our integrity and act as the world does. *Integrity* is "a firm adherence to a code or standard of values." Our code is the Word of God. There are certain things we wouldn't even think of doing, but there are too many compromises, even in the lives of God's people. There are things we do that Jesus would not do, and He is our standard of integrity.

Integrity is being committed to a life of excellence, as our God is excellent. It is doing the right thing every time, no matter what it costs us.

In the body of Christ, we must guard against having leaves without the fruit (Matthew 21:9)—counterfeit spirituality, empty talk, and lifeless formulas.

GOD'S WORD FOR YOU

Depart from evil and do good; seek, inquire for, and crave peace and pursue (go after) it!

PSALM 34:14

THE POWER OF P

David instructs us to pursue peace, go after it. If we want to be in the flow of (it's never going to happen if we are const and stressed out in our lives. If that is true o ife, you may need to cut a few things out of your life.

If you want the peace of God to permeate your life, you cannot exceed your limits. Nobody says you have to do all the things you are doing. Start looking at your life, figure out the commitments that are not bearing any fruit, and start pruning them. You are the one who makes your schedule, and you are the only one who can change it.

It is so important not to overcommit yourself. You need to follow God's leading as to what you are involved in and where you are to use your energy. That includes commitments to your children. Kids don't have to do everything they want to do, and they can't be allowed to control you and your family.

Satan will work overtime to get us to lose our peace and take us away from our faith. Rest in the assurance that God is with us in all that we face.

We must learn to say yes when God says yes and no when He says no. Only as we are obedient to His leading will we be able to walk in spiritual power.

GOD'S WORD FOR YOU

So get rid of all uncleanness and the rampant outgrowth of wickedness, and in a humble (gentle, modest) spirit receive and welcome the Word which implanted and rooted [in your hearts] contains the power to save your souls.

JAMES 1:21

For the Word that God speaks is alive and full of power [making it active, operative, energizing, and effective]; it is sharper than any two-edged sword, penetrating to the dividing line of the breath of life (soul) and [the immortal] spirit, and of joints and marrow [of the deepest parts of our nature], exposing and sifting and analyzing and judging the very thoughts and purposes of the heart.

HEBREWS 4:12

POWER IN THE WORD

Once a person is filled with the Holy Spirit, God is not finished with him. He is just beginning. The tool the Holy Spirit uses to powerfully bring about the transformation of our characters is the Word of God.

The devil's work in the believer's life is based upon deception, which results when lies are believed. As long as I believe the wrong thing, I remain deceived and powerless. When God's Word of truth uncovers those lies, the truth sets us free.

Only the Word of God has this power, and only God can change us. The Word exposes wrong motives, wrong thoughts, and wrong words. Truth can set us free from guilt, self-rejection, condemnation, self-hatred, the works of the flesh, and every lie that we have bought into and brought into our lives. God is out to save and free our entire soul from corruption.

A sword in the sheath is of no value. It must be wielded and appropriately used. The Word of God is the believer's sword, and we must learn to apply it daily, getting it down in our heart, and speaking it out our mouth. The believer who does that is a major threat to Satan and a powerhouse for God.

Love the Word, study the Word, learn the Word.

GOD'S WORD FOR YOU

. . . let everyone who is godly pray—pray to You in a time when You may be found; surely when the great waters [of trial] overflow, they shall not reach [the spirit in] him.

PSALM 32:6

He who dwells in the secret place of the Most High shall remain stable and fixed under the shadow of the Almighty [Whose power no foe can withstand].

PSALM 91:1

℘OWER IN PRAYER

It's simple: If you don't spend time with God, you are cutting yourself off from His power. David tells us that it is in the secret place of the presence of God that we are protected. When we spend time with the Lord in prayer and in His Word, we are in the secret place. It is a place of peace and security where we can give Him our cares and trust Him to take care of us.

We really need to understand the awesomeness of God's presence and what is available to us as believers. Why in the world would we not want to spend time with God? Even Jesus would get up early in the morning to be alone with God. He knew the value of being in the presence of God.

Just dedicate a portion of your time to spend with God. Try not to be legalistic about it, but do try to be as regular with it as you can. Take time to read the Bible and any other Christian books that minister to you. Talk to God. Sometimes you may want to listen to Christian music and worship; other times you may just want to sit there and enjoy the silence. Open up your heart and let His presence into your life.

Spending time in the secret place of His presence changes you from what you are to what only He can make you to be.

GOD'S WORD FOR YOU

[The Servant of God says] The Lord God has given Me the tongue of a disciple and of one who is taught, that I should know how to speak a word in season to him who is weary. He wakens Me morning by morning, He wakens My ear to hear as a disciple [as one who is taught].

ISAIAH 50:4

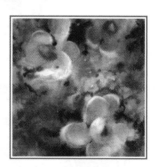

POWER IN WORDS

Words are awesome. Words are containers for power. God created the earth with His words (Hebrews 11:3). The Holy Spirit changes lives with words. People are encouraged or defeated because of words. Marriages break up because people don't say the right words.

Jesus said that His words are spirit, and they are life (John 6:63). But words can also speak death to you by speaking words that put a heaviness on you.

We need to learn to use our mouth for its God-intended purpose. He gave it to us to love people through our encouraging, positive, life-giving words. He gave it to us to give Him praise and thanks. Speaking the right word to a person at the right time can turn their whole life around. Words are powerful.

This is why knowing the Word of God is so important. We need to study it, learn it, and then speak it out according to our situations and needs. For instance, if you feel depressed, don't say, "I'm depressed." Take hold of the Word and say, "Why are you so downcast, O my soul? Put your hope in God." You will be absolutely amazed at how your life will change if you change the way you talk.

Choose to be God's mouthpiece
and close the door to the devil.

BEARING
SPIRITUAL
FRUIT

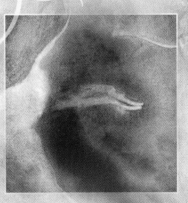

The great responsibility attached to Christianity is to walk in integrity — to "walk the walk," even when nobody notices.

GOD'S WORD FOR YOU

Beware of false prophets, who come to you dressed as sheep, but inside they are devouring wolves.

You will fully recognize them by their fruits. Do people pick grapes from thorns, or figs from thistles?

Even so, every healthy (sound) tree bears good fruit [worthy of admiration], but the sickly (decaying, worthless) tree bears bad (worthless) fruit.

A good (healthy) tree cannot bear bad (worthless) fruit, nor can a bad (diseased) tree bear excellent fruit [worthy of admiration].

Every tree that does not bear good fruit is cut down and cast into the fire.

Therefore, you will fully know them by their fruits.

MATTHEW 7:15–20

six

BEARING SPIRITUAL FRUIT

uring my first few years of ministry, I spent a lot of my prayer time asking God for the special endowments of the gifts of the Holy Spirit to operate through me. To be a powerful minister, I certainly needed them. We all need them. But I didn't give much thought to the fruit of the Spirit. Then one day the Lord impressed upon me, "Joyce, if you would have put even one half as much energy and time into praying about and trying to develop the fruit of the Spirit as you have the gifts, you'd already have both."

As Christians, many of us pray that God will move powerfully through us to help others, and God wants us to pray this way. He has made available to us special endowments of supernatural energy that the Bible calls *spiritual gifts* to use for that very purpose. But I believe our first priority should be developing the fruit of the Spirit.

We are known by our fruit, not by our gifts. We are known to be Jesus' followers by our love for one another, and by our fruit Jesus is known. A display of the fruit of the Spirit, the nature of God, is a display of the character of Jesus Christ.

When people taste the fruit in us and see it is good, they want to find the Source of this fruit—this tree of life. We must show people that what we have is real before they will listen to what we say.

GOD'S WORD FOR YOU

But the fruit of the [Holy] Spirit [the work which His presence within accomplishes] is love, joy (gladness), peace, patience (an even temper, forbearance), kindness, goodness (benevolence), faithfulness,

Gentleness (meekness, humility), self-control (self-restraint, continence). Against such things there is no law [that can bring a charge].

GALATIANS 5:22–23

THE FRUIT OF THE SPIRIT

We are to go out into the world and let the Holy Spirit flow through us to show God's love—His joy, peace, patience, kindness, goodness, faithfulness, gentleness, and self-control—and help people with His gifts. By focusing on the importance God places on developing the fruit of His Spirit, we will find that a door for the release of our gifts will swing wide open.

When the Holy Spirit lives inside us, we have everything He has. His fruit is in us. The seed has been planted. We must allow the seed of the fruit to grow up and mature in us by cultivating it.

We can cultivate all the fruit by focusing on love and self-control, the first and last in the list. All of the fruit issue from love and actually are a form of love, but they are kept in place by self-control. If you are concentrating on developing the fruit of love, you won't become impatient or unkind with people. You will be good to them, supportive and faithful. Self-control helps us to make those little choices throughout the day to respond with the fruit, and soon we form a habit. If you continue to cultivate this habit, you will grow the fruit into an exceptional life in the Spirit.

When our fruit is "squeezed," and we get caught off guard, we discover how undeveloped our fruit is.

GOD'S WORD FOR YOU

Such hope never disappoints or deludes or shames us, for God's love has been poured out in our hearts through the Holy Spirit Who has been given to us.

ROMANS 5:5

And this I pray: that your love may abound yet more and more and extend to its fullest development in knowledge and all keen insight [that your love may display itself in greater depth of acquaintance and more comprehensive discernment] . . .

PHILIPPIANS 1:9

THE POWER OF LOVE

Even when we operate in the greater spiritual gifts, but without love, we are nothing but a big noise or someone who isn't doing anyone any good! Love is not theory or talk, but deeds. Love is actions, doing what needs to be done in every situation.

Concentrate on your love walk and examine your life—your attitudes, your thought life, what you say, how you treat people. How kind are you to people? What are you doing for people? How are you treating people who aren't treating you nicely? Our flesh may not always feel like loving others, but if we want to walk in spiritual power and defeat the enemy, we must say, "It is no longer I who live, but Christ the Messiah lives in me" (Galatians 2:20).

To abound in love is the most excellent thing we can do. And we must do everything with an excellent spirit. We cannot be an excellent person and not walk in love. How can we say that we are walking in love if we are not treating people excellently?

You have the Holy Spirit's power to do what is right—not just what you feel like doing.

Some people feel they need to blow their own horn with their gifts. They don't—they just need to learn to walk in love. The tree is known and judged by its fruit.

GOD'S WORD FOR YOU

He who has no rule over his own spirit is like a city that is broken down and without walls.

PROVERBS 25:28

THE POWER OF SELF-CONTROL

In the world today, Christianity doesn't have a great reputation. The attitude people have about Christians can be painful sometimes because they see us from the world's perspective. But another part of it is, Christians often don't always live up to what they say they believe.

We will not operate in any of the fruit of the Spirit or walk in the power of God without self-control. The fruit of the Spirit is not about how we feel, but about what we choose to do. God gives us self-control so we can discipline ourselves. Without self-control, we cannot have the things we desire.

God wants to help us discipline our thoughts and our mouth. You may feel as though you don't have any discipline or control, but you do! If the Spirit of God lives in you, there it is. God has given us a spirit of power and of love and of a calm and well-balanced mind and discipline and self-control (2 Timothy 1:7).

In the presence of God we need the love of Christ to constrain us and grip our hearts. May all we do and say become an expression of the loving heart of God.

If feelings are your motto in life, then you can stamp disaster across your life. You will not experience victory and make decisions to do what you know you should do.

GOD'S WORD FOR YOU

So that the righteous and just requirement of the Law might be fully met in us who live and move not in the ways of the flesh but in the ways of the Spirit [our lives governed not by the standards and according to the dictates of the flesh, but controlled by the Holy Spirit].

For those who are according to the flesh and are controlled by its unholy desires set their minds on and pursue those things which gratify the flesh, but those who are according to the Spirit and are controlled by the desires of the Spirit set their minds on and seek those things which gratify the [Holy] Spirit.

ROMANS 8:4–5

WALK IN THE SPIRIT

Spiritual power comes with a price tag. In order to walk in the Spirit, we must say no to some things to which we would rather say yes, and yes to some things to which we would rather say no. We must follow the prompting of the Holy Spirit through our own spirit.

To walk in the Spirit requires that we stay filled with the Spirit. This is accomplished by continually choosing right thoughts, conversation, companionship, music, entertainment, etc.

To do God's will, we must be ready to suffer. If our flesh desires to walk one way and God's Spirit is leading us another way, a willful decision to be obedient will provoke suffering in the flesh.

The good news is, if we choose to walk in the Spirit daily, we will die to self-centeredness and gain freedom to serve God. We will experience righteousness, peace, and joy in the Holy Spirit. We will live in victory no matter what comes against us. That's living in power!

Invest in your future: Walk in the Spirit.
Start making right choices. Be persistent
and expect to be blessed.

GOD'S WORD FOR YOU

And do not grieve the Holy Spirit of God [do not offend or vex or sadden Him], by Whom you were sealed (marked, branded as God's own, secured) for the day of redemption (of final deliverance through Christ from evil and the consequences of sin).

EPHESIANS 4:30

Do Not Grieve the Spirit

I take a verse such as Ephesians 4:30 very seriously. I do not want to grieve the Holy Spirit, but how do I avoid doing it? Reading the verses surrounding it makes it clear that one thing that grieves the Holy Spirit is for people to mistreat one another. In verse 29 we are encouraged to edify others with the words of our mouth. Verse 31 exhorts us not to be bitter, angry, or contentious and to beware of slander, spite, and ill will. Then in verse 32 we are told to be kind to one another, forgiving readily and freely.

It comes back to our love walk and how the Holy Spirit has shed abroad the love of God in our hearts. It is He Who teaches us, convicting us of wrong conduct when we mistreat others. It is He Who works in us to give us a tender heart. Pray for such a heart.

When I realized that it grieved the Holy Spirit when I was sharp or hateful with someone, or when I stayed angry at someone, I began to take that kind of behavior more seriously. I also realized that what I was doing made me feel grieved as well. It made me feel sad or depressed, or I had a sense that something just wasn't right. All such disobedience is sin and grieves the Spirit, cutting off our spiritual power.

I have found the secret to being happy
all the time — it is to walk in love.

119

GOD'S WORD FOR YOU

Thank [God] in everything [no matter what the circumstances may be, be thankful and give thanks], for this is the will of God for you [who are] in Christ Jesus [the Revealer and Mediator of that will].

Do not quench (suppress or subdue) the [Holy] Spirit;

Do not spurn the gifts and utterances of the prophets [do not depreciate prophetic revelations nor despise inspired instruction or exhortation or warning].

But test and prove all things [until you can recognize] what is good; [to that] hold fast.

1 THESSALONIANS 5:18–21

Do Not Quench the Spirit

Paul tells us not to quench, suppress, or subdue the Holy Spirit. According to *Webster's*, *to quench* means to "put out," *to suppress* means "to check or stop (a natural flow)," and *to subdue* means "to make less intense." If we quench a fire, we put it out or extinguish it. We do not want to quench the Holy Spirit; instead, we want to make sure we do everything we can to increase His activity and flow in our life.

The previous verses in 1 Thessalonians give us rich insight into walking in spiritual power. From these Scriptures, it is clear that our attitude is very important. It is all about how we act, the behavior patterns we display. Our attitude involves our character, and our character begins with our thoughts.

It quenches the Spirit when we have a bad attitude such as bitterness, anger, unforgiveness, spitefulness, disrespect, vengefulness, a lack of appreciation, and the list goes on and on. The Holy Spirit flows through a godly attitude, not an ungodly one.

Regularly examine your heart and guard it with all diligence (Proverbs 4:23). It's your life source.

If we are smart enough not to swallow poison, we should also be intelligent enough not to allow Satan to poison our mind, attitude, and ultimately our life.

GOD'S WORD FOR YOU

That is why I would remind you to stir up (rekindle the embers of, fan the flame of, and keep burning) the [gracious] gift of God, [the inner fire] that is in you by means of the laying on of my hands [with those of the elders at your ordination].

For God did not give us a spirit of timidity (of cowardice, of craven and cringing and fawning fear), but [He has given us a spirit] of power and of love and of calm and well-balanced mind and discipline and self-control.

2 TIMOTHY 1:6–7

*K*EEP MOVING FORWARD

In our spiritual lives we are either aggressively going forward on purpose, or we are slipping backward. There is no such thing as dormant Christianity. We cannot put our Christian walk or spiritual power on hold. It is vital to keep pressing on. That is why Timothy was instructed to fan the flame and rekindle the fire that once burned in him.

Evidently, Timothy had taken a step backward, perhaps via fear. Anytime we get into fear, we begin to become immobile instead of active. Fear freezes us in place, so to speak; it prevents progress.

It is certainly easy to understand why Timothy may have lost his courage and confidence. It was a time of extreme persecution, and his mentor Paul was in jail. What if the same happened to him?

Yet Paul strongly encouraged Timothy to stir himself up, get back on track, remember the call on his life, resist fear, and remember that God had given him a spirit of power and of love and of a sound mind. All of this had come to him when he received the fullness of the Holy Spirit.

If we intend to stay stirred up in the Holy Spirit, we must choose our thoughts and words carefully.

GOD'S WORD FOR YOU

*But I say, walk and live [habitually] in the [Holy]
Spirit [responsive to and controlled and guided by the
Spirit]; then you will certainly not gratify the cravings
and desires of the flesh (of human nature without God).*

GALATIANS 5:16

Always Be Led by the Spirit

Paul did not say the desires or the lusts of the flesh would die or no longer exist for the children of God. He said that we must choose to be led by the Holy Spirit, and by making that choice, we would not fulfill the lusts of the flesh that continually tempt us.

There are many things available to lead us—other people, the devil and his demons, the flesh (our own body, mind, will, or emotions), or the Holy Spirit. There are many voices in the world that are speaking to us, and often several at the same time.

It is imperative that we learn how to be led by the Holy Spirit. He alone knows the will of God and is sent to dwell in each of us to aid us in being all God has designed us to be and to have all God wants us to have. Being led by the Spirit means He leads us by peace and by wisdom, as well as by the Word of God. He speaks in a still, small voice in our heart or what we often call "the inward witness." Those who want to walk in spiritual power must learn to follow the inward witness and to respond quickly.

The Holy Spirit lives in each of us to help us! We should lift up our entire life daily and say with all our might, "Holy Spirit, You are welcome to move in power in my life!"

JOYCE MEYER

Joyce Meyer has been teaching the Word of God
since 1976 and in full-time ministry since 1980. She
is the bestselling author of over 54 inspirational
books, including *Secrets to Exceptional Living*, *The Joy
of Believing Prayer*, and *Battlefield of the Mind*, as well
as over 240 audiocassette albums and over 90 videos.
Joyce's *Life In The Word* radio and television
programs are broadcast around the world, and she
travels extensively conducting "Life In The Word"
conferences. Joyce and her husband, Dave, are
the parents of four grown children and make
their home in St. Louis, Missouri.

Additional copies of this book are available from your local bookstore.

If this book has changed your life, we would like to hear from you.

Please write us at:

Joyce Meyer Ministries
P.O. Box 655 • Fenton, MO 63026

or call: (636) 349-0303

Internet Address: www.joycemeyer.org

In Canada, write: Joyce Meyer Ministries Canada, Inc.
Lambeth Box 1300 • London, ON N6P 1T5

or call: (636) 349-0303

In Australia, write: Joyce Meyer Ministries—Australia
Locked Bag 77 • Mansfield Delivery Centre
Queensland 4122

or call: (07) 3349 1200

In England, write: Joyce Meyer Ministries
P.O. Box 1549 • Windsor • SL4 1GT

or call: 01753 831102

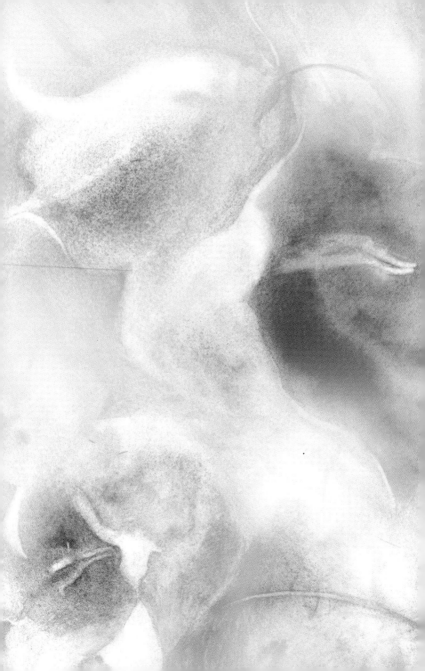